Torque brims with excitement perfect for thrill-seekers of all kinds. Discover daring survival skills, explore uncharted worlds, and marvel at mighty engines and extreme sports. In *Torque* books, anything can happen. Are you ready?

This edition first published in 2026 by Bellwether Media, Inc.

No part of this publication may be reproduced in whole or in part without written permission of the publisher. For information regarding permission, write to Bellwether Media, Inc., Attention: Permissions Department, 3500 American Blvd W, Suite 150, Bloomington, MN 55431.

Library of Congress Cataloging-in-Publication Data

Names: Nguyen, Suzane, author.
Title: Blackpink / by Suzane Nguyen.
Description: Minneapolis, MN : Bellwether Media, 2026. | Series: Music superstars | Includes bibliographical references and index. | Audience: Ages 7-12 | Audience: Grades 4-6 | Summary: "Engaging images accompany information about BLACKPINK. The combination of high-interest subject matter and light text is intended for students in grades 3 through 7"- Provided by publisher.
Identifiers: LCCN 2025001584 (print) | LCCN 2025001585 (ebook) | ISBN 9798893044997 (library binding) | ISBN 9798893046373 (ebook)
Subjects: LCSH: Blackpink (Musical group)–Juvenile literature. | Women singers–Korea (South)–Biography–Juvenile literature. | Singers–Korea (South)–Biography–Juvenile literature. | Girl groups (Musical groups)–Korea (South)–Juvenile literature.
Classification: LCC ML3930.B579 N48 2026 (print) | LCC ML3930.B579 (ebook) | DDC 782.4216/3095195 [B]–dc23/eng/20250115
LC record available at https://lccn.loc.gov/2025001584
LC ebook record available at https://lccn.loc.gov/2025001585

Text copyright © 2026 by Bellwether Media, Inc. TORQUE and associated logos are trademarks and/or registered trademarks of Bellwether Media, Inc. Bellwether Media is a division of FlutterBee Education Group.

Editor: Rachael Barnes   Designer: Josh Brink

Printed in the United States of America, North Mankato, MN.

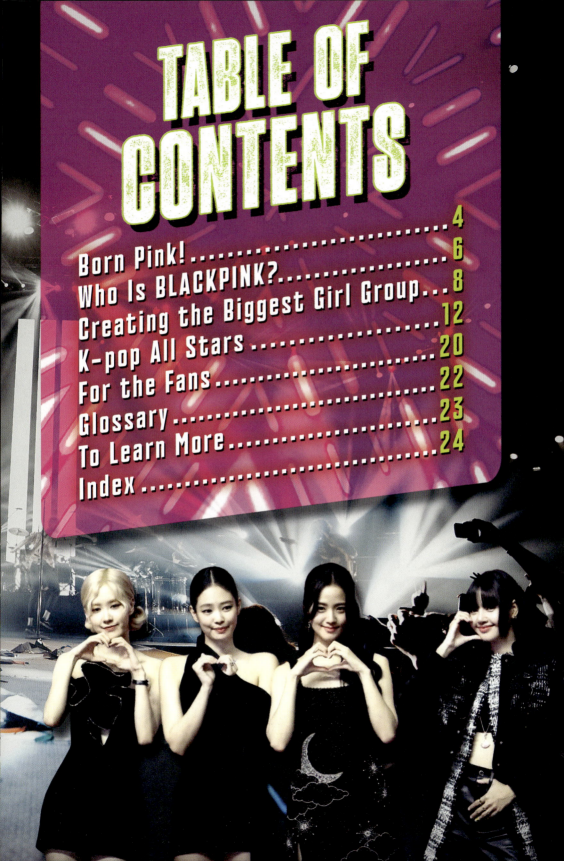

TABLE OF CONTENTS

Born Pink!	4
Who Is BLACKPINK?	6
Creating the Biggest Girl Group	8
K-pop All Stars	12
For the Fans	20
Glossary	22
To Learn More	23
Index	24

BORN PINK!

It is 2022 and the Born Pink world tour has been performing around the globe. Tonight, BLACKPINK takes the stage in Los Angeles, California!

Pink lights flash as a rock beat fills the stadium. BLACKPINK strikes a pose. They dance together and sing their hit song "Pink Venom." Fireworks light up the stage as the girls sing their final note. Everyone cheers!

WHO IS BLACKPINK?

BLACKPINK is a **K-pop** group from South Korea. They perform pop, hip-hop, and electronic dance music (EDM). The four-member girl group has broken many records and won many awards.

BLACKPINK

Members: Jennie, Jisoo, Lisa, and Rosé

Date Debuted: August 2016

Types of Music: pop, hip-hop, EDM

First Hit: "Boombayah"

BLACKPINK AWARDED FOR CLIMATE CHANGE WORK

BLACKPINK has also worked with the **United Nations**. They speak out to educate people about **climate change**.

CREATING THE BIGGEST GIRL GROUP

Each member took different paths to join the group. Jennie listened to K-pop growing up. She, Rosé, and Jisoo all loved to sing. Rosé learned to play piano and guitar. Lisa became known for her dancing.

A company called YG Entertainment wanted to create an **international** girl group. The four girls were selected and trained with the company.

FROM NINE TO FOUR

There were supposed to be nine members in BLACKPINK!

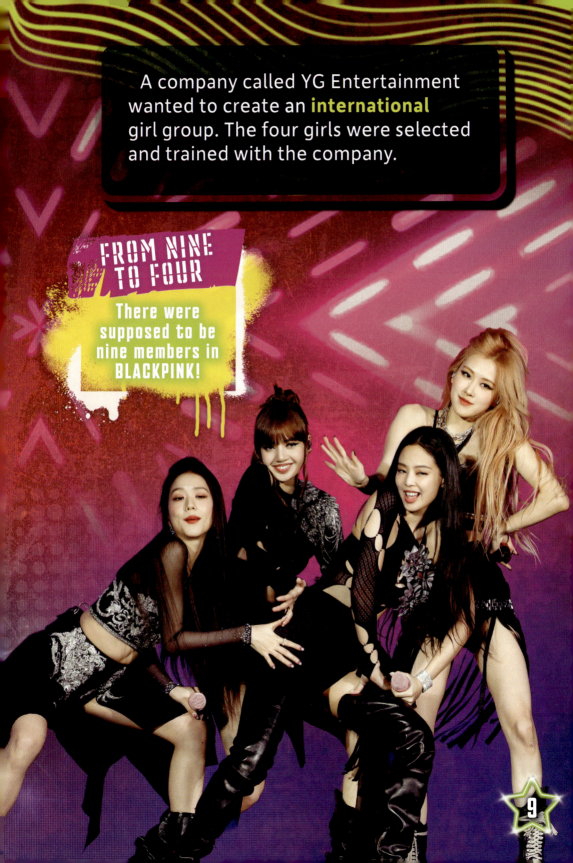

Jennie was the first member to join YG. She **auditioned** and began training. Lisa attended an audition in Thailand. She was selected and moved to South Korea to train.

FAVORITES

Food
Rosé likes Korean corn dogs

Color
Lisa likes yellow

Artist
Jennie likes Rihanna

Disney Movie
Jisoo likes *Tangled*

Jisoo acted in commercials before she was asked to join YG. Rosé attended an audition in Australia. After years of training, YG put the four together. The group was formed!

K-POP ALL STARS

BLACKPINK **debuted** in 2016 with their **EP** *Square One*. It had two songs, "Boombayah" and "Whistle." Both were top-ranking songs on the *Billboard* World Digital Song Sales chart.

TIMELINE

— 2016 —
BLACKPINK debuts with their songs "Whistle" and "Boombayah"

— 2018 —
BLACKPINK releases their EP *Square Up*

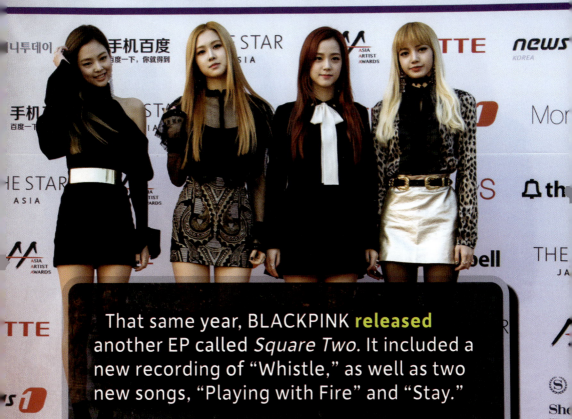

That same year, BLACKPINK **released** another EP called *Square Two*. It included a new recording of "Whistle," as well as two new songs, "Playing with Fire" and "Stay."

— 2020 —
BLACKPINK releases their first album, *The Album*

— 2022 —
BLACKPINK begins their 11-month-long Born Pink world tour

— 2023 —
BLACKPINK becomes the first K-pop group to be a main act at Coachella Valley Music and Arts Festival

BLACKPINK had a big year in 2018. They released *Square Up*. It included four new songs. The EP did well, topping the *Billboard* World Album chart.

AWARDS

as of February 2025

11 MAMA Awards

1 *Billboard* Music Award

4 MTV Video Music Awards

3 People's Choice Awards

YOUTUBE RECORD BREAKERS

"DDU-DU DDU-DU" is the most viewed YouTube video by a K-pop group. It has over 2.2 billion views!

Their song "DDU-DU DDU-DU" made it onto the *Billboard* Hot 100 chart. It was also one of the first K-pop songs to sell over 500,000 copies!

BLACKPINK hit the road for their first world tour in 2018. The In Your Area world tour was popular!

The group released another EP in 2019. Their new song, "Kill This Love" was a hit! Soon, well-known artists wanted to work with them. BLACKPINK **collaborated** with Lady Gaga and Selena Gomez in 2020!

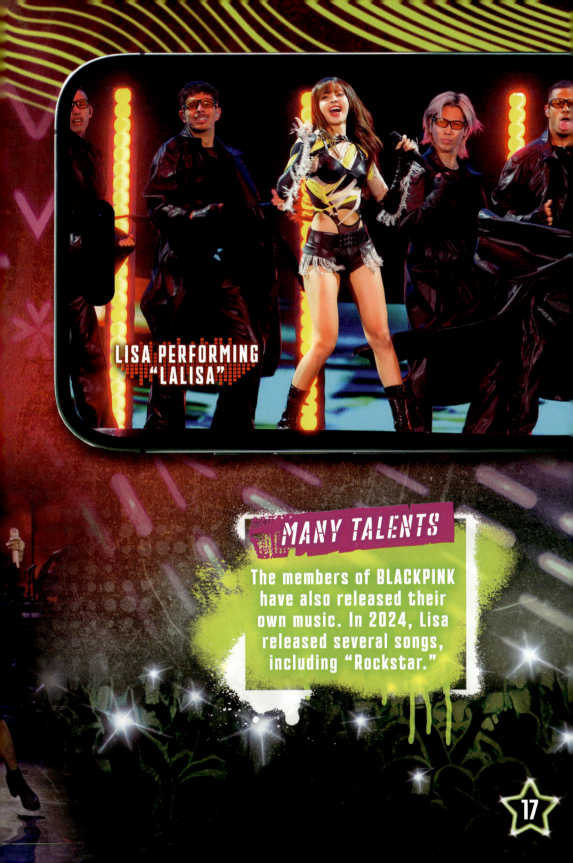

LISA PERFORMING "LALISA"

MANY TALENTS

The members of BLACKPINK have also released their own music. In 2024, Lisa released several songs, including "Rockstar."

BLACKPINK released their first album in 2020 called *The Album*. One of its songs won an **MTV Video Music Award**!

THE MAIN ACT

In 2023, BLACKPINK was the first K-pop group to be the main performance at Coachella Valley Music and Arts Festival!

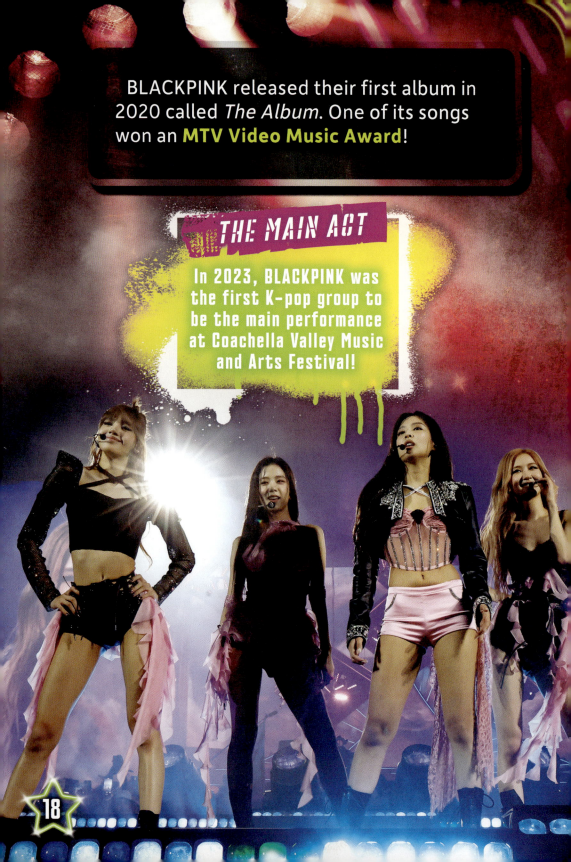

In 2022, BLACKPINK released their second album, *Born Pink*. The same year, they went on an 11-month-long world tour. It became the highest-earning world tour by a girl group ever.

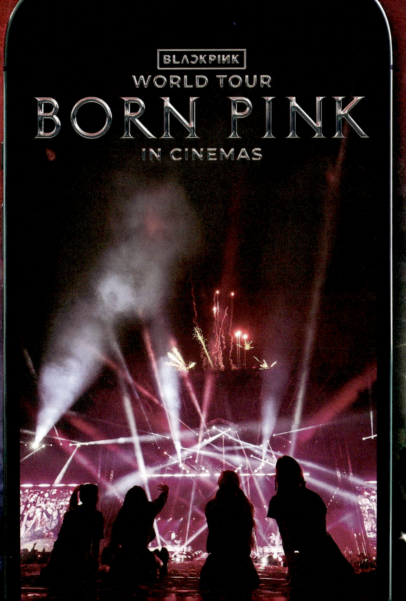

FOR THE FANS

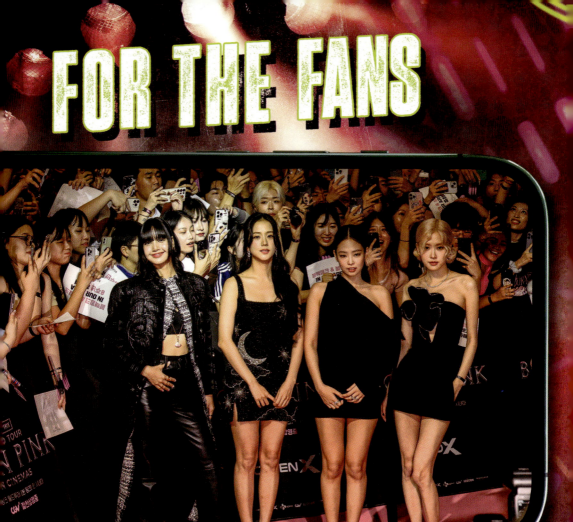

BLACKPINK fans are called Blinks. Many fans are young women. BLACKPINK's songs **inspire** confidence and self-love.

BLACKPINK has plans to release new songs and go on a world tour in 2025. Blinks cannot wait to see more of this talented group!

TOUGH AND SWEET

BLACKPINK chose their name to show who they are. Pink relates to their girly side. Black shows their toughness.

PLAYLIST

"Whistle" (2016)

"Ddu-Du Ddu-Du" (2018)

"Ice Cream" (2020)

"How You Like That" (2020)

"Pink Venom" (2022)

21

GLOSSARY

auditioned—tried out for a role

Billboard—related to a well-known music news magazine and website that ranks songs and albums

climate change—a human-caused change in Earth's weather that leads to warming temperatures

collaborated—worked with others to create something

debuted—was introduced or released for the first time

EP—a music recording that is shorter than an album but has more songs than a single; EP stands for extended play.

inspire—to give someone an idea about what to do or create

international—known in many countries around the world

K-pop—related to pop music that comes from South Korea

MTV Video Music Award—a yearly award presented for achievements in music videos, as well as the top songs, artists, and performances

released—made music available for listening

United Nations—an organization that aims to protect the peace and safety of people around the world

TO LEARN MORE

AT THE LIBRARY

Bolte, Mari. *What You Never Knew About Blackpink*. North Mankato, Minn.: Capstone Press, 2025.

Brown, Helen. *Blackpink: Queens of K-pop*. New York, N.Y.: Sterling Publishing Co., 2020.

Rose, Rachel. *Blackpink: K-pop Sensations*. Minneapolis, Minn.: Lerner Publications, 2025.

ON THE WEB

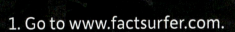

Factsurfer.com gives you a safe, fun way to find more information.

1. Go to www.factsurfer.com.

2. Enter "BLACKPINK" into the search box and click 🔍.

3. Select your book cover to see a list of related content.

INDEX

acting, 11
albums, 14, 18, 19
awards, 6, 15, 18
Billboard, 12, 14, 15
Blinks, 20
childhood, 8, 10, 11
Coachella Valley Music and Arts Festival, 18
dancing, 5, 8
EPs, 12, 13, 14, 16
fans, 20
favorites, 11
Gomez, Selena, 16
instruments, 8
Lady Gaga, 16
members, 6, 8, 9, 10, 11, 17
name, 21
playlist, 21
profile, 7
records, 6, 15, 18, 19
sales, 12, 15
songs, 5, 12, 13, 14, 15, 16, 17, 18, 20
South Korea, 6, 10
timeline, 12–13
tours, 4, 5, 16, 19, 20
types of music, 6, 8, 15, 18
United Nations, 7
YG Entertainment, 9, 10, 11
YouTube, 15

The images in this book are reproduced through the courtesy of: Emma McIntyre/ Getty Images, front cover, pp. 10, 21; Catsense, front cover (light effect); Taya Ovod, pp. 2-3; TV10/ Wikipedia, p. 3; Christopher Polk/ Penske Media/ Getty Images, pp. 4, 5; Emma McIntyre/ Getty Images for Coachella/ Getty Images, p. 6; Victoria Jones/ Alamy, p. 7; DELICATO/ Wikipedia, p. 7 (VIP pass); Kevin Mazur/ Getty Images, p. 8; Frazer Harrison/ Getty Images, pp. 9, 10-11; aperturesound, p. 11 (Korean corn dog); Elena11, p. 11 (paint swatch); ABACAPRESS/ Alamy, p. 11 (Rihanna); DatBot/ Wikipedia, p. 11 (*Tangled*); ED JONES/ AFP/ Getty Images, pp. 12-13; BWM, pp. 12-13, 21; YG Entertainment/ Wikipedia, p. 13; Visual China Group, pp. 14-15; MOHD FYROL/ AFP/ Getty Images, p. 15 (MAMA Awards); Kathy Hutchins, p. 15 (*Billboard* Music Award); WFDJ_Stock, p. 15 (MTV Video Music Awards); s_bukley, p. 15 (People's Choice Awards); Natt Lim/ Getty Images for Coachella/ Getty Images, p. 16; zz/XPX/STAR MAX/IPx/ AP Images, p. 17; Frazer Harrison/ Getty Images for Coachella/ Getty Images, pp. 18, 23; TCD/Prod.DB/ Alamy, p. 19; ANTHONY WALLACE/ AFP/ Getty Images, p. 20.

24